RETRO GAMES

Profiling the best titles from the golden age of gaming

MARTY ALLEN

DOG 'n' BONE

DEDICATION

Dedicated with admiration, gratitude, and respect for Satoru Iwatc
(1959–2015), Nintendo President, game maker, fan, and more:
"*Above all, video games are meant to just be one thing:
Fun for everyone.*"

Published in 2018 by Dog 'n' Bone Books
An imprint of Ryland Peters & Small Ltd

20–21 Jockey's Fields   341 E 116th St
London WC1R 4BW   New York, NY 10029

www.rylandpeters.com

10 9 8 7 6 5 4 3 2 1

Text © Marty Allen 2018
Design © Dog 'n' Bone Books 2018

A CIP catalog record for this book is
available from the Library of Congress
and the British Library.

ISBN: 978 1 911026 62 4

Printed in China

Editor: Caroline West
Designer: Jerry Goldie
Photography credits: All images from
www.iStock.com and www.Shutterstock.com,
except for console images by Evan Amos sourced
from Wikipedia.com.

CONTENTS

PRESS START

All I wanted for Christmas in 1985 was a Nintendo Entertainment System
I did not get it. Instead I got a note from the big guy, with an oddly familia
script explaining that the elves were backed up, but they'd bring me my
heart's desire in a few weeks. I counted the days—two weeks was two
years to a 7-year-old—and when the Nintendo arrived, my clammy little
hands couldn't shred the box and plug in the wires fast enough. With the
push of a power button, our dusty den was transformed into a palace
of pixelated wonders. I pressed the A-button, steered right, and made a
plumber hit his head on some bricks. This moment forever sits cemented in
my brain, synonymous with both joy and discovery. But when does such a
moment transform from memory into nostalgia? It's a subtle shift. We long
for the pixelated past because that time was important to our lives. These
retro memories matter. But why?

Are video games art? Are they entertainment? Are they a story-telling
medium or a fancy board game? Are they a scourge on the mind or a
gateway to a new dimension? Lara Croft and Bowser don't care. We save
Hyrule, destroyed Mother Brain, and blew up zombies in Raccoon City
without making such lofty inquiries. We lost hours in bedrooms, gained
allies and enemies among our families, and came out the other side swea
and smiling. Today, it is clear that video games have stuck around long
enough to become a part of our culture. But, more importantly, we grew
up together.

Video games matter, and so does the time we played them. We move
pixels about a screen to solve pretend problems, and those moments stay
with us. Grab the mushroom, punch the dinosaur, fit the puzzle piece in
its hole, and save the day. Like rollercoasters and ice cream, interactive
gaming is a wonder of human innovation, and these dancing pixels have
been with us, lighting up our lives.

I've played nearly every game in this book. I didn't play them for research
or in order to write this book. I played them because I love video games
and they matter to me, and I love thinking about the joy I've found in
playing them. So do you. Let's share some memories, shall we?

A FEW NOTES

RELEASE DATES

Whenever possible, game release dates have been verified using two reputable sources, but are sometimes approximate to give a sense of where they exist on the broader timeline. During earlier console generations, games were often released first in Japan, then in the States, then in Europe. For the sake of clarity and space (and with the exception of major console releases), the cited dates are North American.

CREATIVE CREDITS

Video games are a young medium, and it often takes many people to make them. Where possible, I've credited the folk who are most closely associated with the creation of a game (as I've best been able to ascertain from at least two reliable sources). It can be difficult to assess who did what. As such it is all too likely that some important names have been left off the lists, while in other cases the credit given doesn't do justice to the broad roles played. All of which is a way of saying that this book is written with the utmost respect for all the people who helped make these wonderful games, and with apologies to those we missed. Thanks, and let us know if your name isn't here.

IMAGES

The astute observer will note that there are no actual pictures of the games I'm talking about. While I'd love to insist that this was an artistic conceit, it has much more to do with mine and my publisher's reasonable and tactful lack of a desire to cross cranky lawyers—we did approach various companies, and emails were either ignored or shoulders were shrugged as to how permissions could be cleared. Creative copyright of images of video games is a real thing, and we are honoring it by not printing images of these games without the permission of their creators. It is my hope that my words have worked in tandem with the design to evoke a symphony of 8-bit memories that transcend or, at the least, honor the source.

NINTENDO ENTERTAINMENT SYSTEM/FAMICOM

RELEASE DATES:

> JAPAN: **JULY, 1983**

> NORTH AMERICA: **OCTOBER, 1985**

> EUROPE: **SEPTEMBER, 1986**

Nintendo saved video games. In 1983, the home console market crashed like a bag of E.T. cartridges thrown from a 40-story window, leaving consumers with a serious aversion to the very words "video game." The previously successful Atari 2600, along with several of its competitors and sequels, had all but disappeared under a glut of bad licensing. Businesses and consumers viewed home consoles as just another passing fad, but Nintendo had other plans. Already an old and experienced toy manufacturer, Nintendo had dabbled in home electronics, at one point nearly partnering with Atari for a console release. That fell through, but The Big N could still sense the market's potential; they knew that they just needed to change the playing field.

It took time, but Nintendo went to great pains to ensure that their new home system would distance itself from "video games" as consumers knew them. Through a focused marketing effort, Nintendo's wizards branded it an "entertainment system" (the Japanese version was called the Famicom, a portmanteau of "Family Computer"), created a front-loading cartridge slot reminiscent of the contemporary VCR, and packaged it with intriguing bells and whistles such as R.O.B. the robot and a light gun. On top of this appealing package, they also implemented a quality-control system to reign in third-party software—previous generations of games saw shovel-ware take over shelves, and Nintendo knew consumers were weary, so the Seal of Approval was born. They understood that games were what sold systems, so they rolled out their own slate of compelling games such as *Duck Hunt* and *Super Mario Bros.* with the launch.

All these games were played on what was arguably their greatest innovation, a simple control pad that was a miniature revolution, introducing the still-standard, four-way directional pad to replace the then-ubiquitous joystick. By the time Mario made his way into the eager hands of a generation, the rest was history. Nintendo had revived gaming, as we know it, though not for the last time.

Super Mario Bros.

> Year: **October, 1985**

> Platform: **Nintendo Entertainment System**

> Developer: **Nintendo**

> Creators: **Shigeru Miyamoto, Takashi Tezuka**

Shigeru Miyamoto said, "A game that keeps a smile on the player's face is a wonderful thing." Few things trigger smiles like the simple joy of seeing a little red plumber hit his head against a question-block in World 1-1 of *Super Mario Bros.* From Koji Kondo's iconic music to the game's improbable use of mushrooms as power-ups, Mario and Luigi not only changed the game, but also saved it with a smile.

With *Super Mario Bros.*, Nintendo took the form of video games and developed it, adding a coat of polish that has become synonymous with their in-house games. In doing so, they launched a mascot and the Nintendo brand into happy homes and the history books. But their innovations, like so much of what Nintendo does, were playful and welcoming. What mattered most was that everyone wanted to pick up and play this game, and that they could. *Super Mario Bros.* is immediately understandable—Mario runs and jumps and stomps on stuff—and every element is crafted with such care and precision that it just made sense. It set the standard that still brings smiles to the faces of gamers today.

THE LEGEND OF ZELDA

> YEAR: **FEBRUARY, 1986**

> PLATFORM: **NINTENDO ENTERTAINMENT SYSTEM**

> DEVELOPER: **NINTENDO**

> CREATORS: **SHIGERU MIYAMOTO, TAKASHI TEZUKA**

Reflecting on his *Zelda* series, Shigeru Miyamoto said, "I think many people dream about becoming heroes." Any child of the 1980s who clutched a golden NES cartridge and burnt down the bushes of Hyrule is living evidence that Miyamoto did his job.

The Legend of Zelda was developed at the same time as *Super Mario Bros.*, a fact that is itself amazing in light of the impact of both games. Miyamoto and his team wanted to separate Zelda from Mario, so they crafted an open-ended fantasy game with an elaborate map, intricate dungeons, and unique monsters. From the first time you dropped a bomb on Dodongo (he dislikes smoke) to the moment you emerged from the Lost Woods (north, west, south, west), *The Legend of Zelda* lived up to its name—it's legendary, and you are the hero. To this day, when a new *Zelda* game is announced, it is cause for the entire gaming community to stop everything it's doing, put on their green tunics, and get ready to be heroes again.

DUCK HUNT

> YEAR: **OCTOBER 1985**

> PLATFORM: **NINTENDO ENTERTAINMENT SYSTEM**

> DEVELOPER: **NINTENDO**

> PRODUCERS: **GUNPEI YOKOI, SHIGERU MIYAMOTO**

Shooting gallery games are as old as the carnival and the arcade. With *Duck Hunt*, Nintendo sought to capitalize on this well-trodden pastime in their new home console, creating the single best reason to have a Nintendo Zapper as part of your gaming arsenal.

In *Duck Hunt*, your task is self-explanatory—point a gun and shoot at ducks (and some occasional target discs). Miss, and you get taunted by a deeply irritating dog. Repeat. The resulting game proved curiously addictive, both because it was included as one of the first pack-ins for the console, but also because, in some primal and ineffable way, it just worked. Those who spent long hours hunting ducks can still hear the lonesome 8-bit bark of the dog, as it flushes your would-be prey, and its deliciously maddening snicker if you fail at your task.

METROID

> YEAR: **AUGUST, 1986**

> PLATFORM: **NINTENDO ENTERTAINMENT SYSTEM**

> DEVELOPER: **NINTENDO**

> PRODUCER: **GUNPEI YOKOI**

> DIRECTOR: **YOSHIO SAKAMOTO**

Nintendo had already found critical and commercial success with *Donkey Kong*, *Super Mario Bros.*, and *The Legend of Zelda*, but they longed for an outer-space adventure with a darker tone. *Metroid* was produced by one of Nintendo's lesser-known early heroes, the late Gunpei Yokoi, who, along with Metroid's talented team, crafted another Nintendo icon.

Heavily inspired by Ridley Scott's film *Alien*, *Metroid*'s moody fusion of an open-world, science-fiction landscape and open-ended discovery changed adventure games. The new concept of a weapons and power-up system that allowed the exploration of areas which initially appeared inaccessible laid the groundwork for a generation of side-scrolling adventure games dubbed *Metroid-vania*, a fusion of this game's name and that of its influential contemporary, *Castlevania*. The enduring *Metroid* franchise inspires some of Nintendo's deepest loyalties. The original is perhaps best remembered for the then-revolutionary ending-reveal that its super-powerful, bounty-hunter protagonist, Samus Aran, had been… spoiler alert… a lady all along!

CONTRA

> YEAR: **FEBRUARY, 1987**

> PLATFORM: **NINTENDO ENTERTAINMENT SYSTEM**

> DEVELOPER: **KONAMI**

> DESIGNER: **SHIGEHARU UMEZAKI**

Contra is as much a game about shirtless mercenaries shooting clever guns at relentless swooping aliens as it is about running and jumping and dying a lot. A classic run-and-gun shooter, *Contra* was ported from a more robust arcade game down to an equally satisfying home version for the NES in 1987. It demonstrated the power of third-party support, while making it possible for two players to scream about their inevitable deaths at the hands of hordes of alien fiends in the comfort of their own homes. Thankfully, *Contra* was also the game to popularize the now culturally pervasive *Konami Code* to help save the day.

Created initially for Konami's *Gradius*, the player inputs "up-up-down-down-left-right-left-right-B-A-start" into the controller. This became the convoluted cheat to end all cheats when it rose to fame with *Contra,* adding 30 entirely necessary extra lives. Rifs and permutations of the *Konami Code* have gone on to feature in nearly every Konami game to date (and countless non-Konami games, movies, songs, novels, and television shows), leaving that string of obscure inputs cemented into the impressionable minds of a sore-thumbed generation.

Punch-Out!!

(Originally Mike Tyson's Punch-Out!!)

> Year: **October, 1987**

> Platform: **Nintendo Entertainment System**

> Developer: **Nintendo**

> Creators: **Genyo Takeda, Minoru Arakawa**

There's still something special about *Punch-Out!!* In this translation from the arcade original, the changes Nintendo made out of necessity managed to craft a compelling and surprisingly strategic boxing simulation that transcends its source material. Instead of the wire-frame dummy and bare-bones story found in the arcade, you step into the little shoes of Little Mac, and make your way up the boxing circuit through a swathe of cartoonish opponents. Rather than simply punching everything in his way, our diminutive hero uses a deceptively simple move-set to break down the patterns of each of his over-the-top pugilist foes in order to score the elusive KO (knockout) or TKO (technical knockout).

Punch-Out!! ends up having as much in common with a puzzle game as it does with a sporting simulation. Top that off with the Rocky-inspired story, as told via training-sequence cutscenes between Little Mac and Doc, and you get the stuff of legend, including unforgettable advice like, "Join the Nintendo Fun Club today, Mac!"

MEGA MAN 2

> YEAR: **DECEMBER, 1988**

> PLATFORM: **NINTENDO ENTERTAINMENT SYSTEM**

> DEVELOPER: **CAPCOM**

> DIRECTOR: **AKIRA KITAMURA**

> ARTIST: **KEIJI INAFUNE**

While the original *Mega Man* defined the formula for its many sequels to come, it was *Mega Man 2* that launched the series to greatness and acclaim. In *Mega Man* games, you are an iconic little blue robot, sent by your creator, Dr. Light, to defeat the evil scientist, Dr. Wily. In order to do so, you must destroy Dr. Wily's robotic creations and take on their powers.

In *Mega Man 2*, those robot foes are Metal Man, Air Man, Bubble Man, Quick Man, Crash Man, Flash Man, Heat Man, and Wood Man, and they are collectively and individually a master class in boss design. Each of their themed worlds functions as the perfect support for this unforgettable action game. While the bosses can be tackled in any order, through trial and error (or with some help from *Nintendo Power*), players eventually discover that each boss has a weakness to another's powers, opening up a preferred progression of robot awesomeness and opening the doors for an unforgettable series.

Ninja Gaiden

(European Release: Shadow Warriors)

> Year: **March, 1989**

> Platform: **Nintendo Entertainment System**

> Developer: **Tecmo**

> Director: **Hideo Yoshizawa (as Sakurazaki)**

"The wind howls as the two dueling ninjas glare at each other in the moonlight." (Prologue, *Ninja Gaiden Instruction Manual*). The dream of becoming a ninja has fueled adolescent fantasies since long before a group of pizza-loving turtles took over the New York sewer system. *Ninja Gaiden* made that katana-swinging aspiration real when Ryu Hyabusa arrived on the NES to avenge his father's death. As it turns out, being a ninja—at least one cast in the world of *Ninja Gaiden*—is extremely hard.

Ninja Gaiden is a celebrated title from the 8-bit era of gaming, but that celebration is often colored with dark memories of game controllers being thrown like frustrated ninja stars due to its high difficulty curve. But players who persevered were rewarded, as *Ninja Gaiden* is also remembered for its pioneering use of cinematic cutscenes to tell Ryu's harrowing tale.

CASTLEVANIA 3

> YEAR: **DECEMBER, 1989**

> PLATFORM: **NINTENDO ENTERTAINMENT SYSTEM**

> DEVELOPER: **KONAMI**

> DIRECTOR: **HITOSHI AKAMATSU**

Everyone loves a good vampire hunt. From the first candle you whip to Dracula's final demise, the original *Castlevania* trilogy is truly special, presenting the ultimate exercise in chasing not only blood-sucking beasts, but also a wonderful menagerie of monsters—all set against an unforgettable, 8-bit, gothic backdrop.

    Castlevania 3 took the best from both of its predecessors, but ends up looking like a super-sized version of the original. The third entry in the series brought together atmosphere, style, and gameplay, leaving the player feeling like the star of a monster-movie journey. As the whip-wielding Trevor Belmont, you must once again climb the castle and slay Dracula, battling as many flying Medusa heads and stacked-up skulls as you can along the winding way. The *Castlevania* trilogy represents a classic corner of gaming history, and *Castlevania 3* is its vampire-slaying pinnacle.

SUPER MARIO BROS. 3

> YEAR: **FEBRUARY, 1990**

> PLATFORM: **NINTENDO ENTERTAINMENT SYSTEM**

> DEVELOPER: **NINTENDO**

> PRODUCER: **SHIGERU MIYAMOTO**

> DIRECTOR: **TAKASHI TEZUKA**

While the original *Super Mario Bros.* transformed gaming forever, Nintendo struggled to find Mario's true sequel. In Japan, the follow-up that would eventually become the *Lost Levels* felt too similar to the original, while in the States, *Super Mario Bros. 2* re-skinned another franchise for a very fun and strange departure, but one that was ultimately more of a side-road for the series. It was this third sequel to the franchise that perfected the formula for fun in video games that still holds today.

Famously introduced in a movie about video games, *The Wizard*, *SMB3* injected Nintendo with a much-needed dose of relevance and held its own as the 16-bit era dawned. An inspiration to a generation of game designers and fans, *SMB3* added flight, countless new attacks and suits, gorgeous worlds, a menagerie of new enemies, and a giant shoe to run around in. The sum total is simply one of the greatest games of all time, and remains the 8-bit measuring stick that all 2D platformers are held against. Fly, Tanooki, fly!

GAME BOY

RELEASE DATES:

> JAPAN: **APRIL, 1989**

> NORTH AMERICA: **JULY, 1989**

> EUROPE: **SEPTEMBER, 1990**

In 1989, Nintendo proved that there was a lucrative market for portable consoles, allowing gamers to play wherever they went. Nintendo has a long history with successful handhelds, its popular stand-alone *Game & Watch* games being some of their earliest successes. But where the *Game & Watch* series had been individual titles, the Game Boy would be its own hardware platform. The original system was shepherded through development by the late Gunpei Yokoi, who'd designed many of Nintendo's early toys and technology. For the Game Boy, his team prioritized practicality and good software in order to ensure its success.

One of the most noteworthy features that set the Game Boy apart was one of its simplest—a strong battery life. Nintendo also made sure that the system launched with a killer app, an excellent new Mario game, *Super Mario Land*. However, it was the surprise hit of another

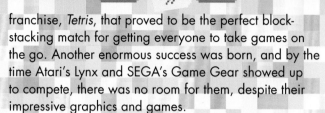

franchise, *Tetris*, that proved to be the perfect block-stacking match for getting everyone to take games on the go. Another enormous success was born, and by the time Atari's Lynx and SEGA's Game Gear showed up to compete, there was no room for them, despite their impressive graphics and games.

The Game Boy would go on to evolve and persist for more than 15 years, introducing smaller and full-color iterations as it grew and setting the stage for Nintendo's next generation of handheld systems, while always prioritizing fun and practicality over technological wizardry to win over the eager hands of gamers on the move.

TETRIS

> YEAR: **JULY, 1989 [FOR GAME BOY]**

> PLATFORM(S): **GAME BOY, NINTENDO ENTERTAINMENT SYSTEM, AND MORE**

> CREATORS: **ALEXEY PAJITNOV, DMITRY PAVLOVSKY, VADIM GERASIMOV**

Tetris is synonymous with video games, and *Tetris* is still fun. The game was originally designed by Russian programmer Alexey Pajitnov, who was inspired by his childhood love of geometric puzzle toys to create a game which tested the artificial intelligence he was working on. It turns out the game he made was as addictive as it was fun. As Henk Rogers, one of *Tetris*'s important early distributors put it, "*Tetris* made Game Boy, and Game Boy made *Tetris*." It wasn't until this compulsive puzzle game was released on the Game Boy as a pack-in in 1989 that it began its ubiquitous life, eventually making appearances on nearly every platform and console to date.

While *Tetris* has gone through a few small evolutions over the years, the core simplicity of turning and stacking up falling blocks to make them fit together remains an enduring favorite for gamers of all ages and nations. It's just like the original box art declares: "From Russia with fun!"

POKÉMON
RED/GREEN/BLUE

> YEAR: **SEPTEMBER 1998**

> PLATFORM: **GAME BOY**

> DEVELOPER: **GAME FREAK**

> DIRECTOR: **SATOSHI SAJIRI**

"Gotta catch 'em all!" An idea originally inspired by series creator Satoshi Sajiri's childhood joy of bug-collecting, in *Pokémon* you capture and befriend strange little monsters, keep them in balls, and make them battle one another. *Pokémon* arrived on Game Boy in 1996 and set the stage for a cultural phenomenon, a craze that has extended into cartoons, movies, a card game, and an endless array of spinoffs and merchandizing.

One of the most enduring brands of our time, *Pokémon*'s world, lore, and list of monsters has grown as the franchise has evolved, but much of what has made the series so appealing was cooked into this, its earliest generation of pocket monsters, many of whom, including Pikachu, Charizard, and Bulbasaur, remain its most iconic creations. The first of the main series of games was, like so many of its sequels, spread across three different-colored versions and featured a fusion of traditional RPG (role-playing game) battling with good old-fashioned monster collection. With over 279 million units sold collectively across the series and its various spinoffs since, it's safe to say that we will never catch them all.

SEGA GENESIS/ MEGA DRIVE

RELEASE DATES:

> JAPAN: **OCTOBER, 1988**

> NORTH AMERICA: **AUGUST, 1989**

> EUROPE: **SEPTEMBER, 1990**

"GENESIS DOES WHAT NINTENDON'T." So read the legendary ad copy for the SEGA Genesis, and in many ways the ALL-CAPS slogan was the all-caps TRUTH. The Genesis (or Mega Drive outside of the US) was not SEGA's first foray into home consoles (nor their last), but it was their most successful and most influential. By 1988, Nintendo controlled the rejuvenated and lucrative home-gaming market and looked unstoppable. But SEGA arrived with its next generation of 16-bit hardware two years ahead of Nintendo, and set out to impress.

Firing off pixelated flares with high-quality ports of its deep roster of popular arcade games such as *Altered Beast*, the Genesis still struggled to get out from under Mario's shadow. However, an orchestrated effort to market itself as a cooler and more grown-up alternative to Nintendo resonated with a generation. SEGA's efforts

to sell to the newly adolescent fan base were buoyed by the many third-party developers who had, until then, been largely pushed out by Nintendo's notoriously rigid standards and practices.

SEGA eventually attracted a number of lucrative movie and sports licenses, as well as more "mature" (read: bloody) versions of games that went cross-platform. This deft mixture of games alongside their spotlight-stealing new mascot, *Sonic the Hedgehog,* turned out to be the winning formula that finally gave Nintendo a run for its bags and bags of money. SEGA's disruptive console sparked the so-called "Console Wars," and changed and matured home gaming. The SEGA Genesis/Mega Drive showed the world that there was room for more than just what Nintendo had to offer, and during its short and glorious reign, SEGA delivered some of the greatest games of its time.

SONIC THE HEDGEHOG

> YEAR: **JUNE, 1991**

> PLATFORM: **SEGA GENESIS/MEGA DRIVE**

> DEVELOPER: **SONIC TEAM**

> DESIGNERS:: **HIROKAZU YASUHARA, NAOTO OHSHIMA**

> PROGRAMMER: **YUJI NAKA**

SEGA needed a mascot to compete with Mario. They'd found some early commercial success for their next-generation competitor with arcade ports, but with the Super Nintendo entering the 16-bit fray, they needed something iconic to challenge Nintendo's beloved plumber. Originally named the less inspiring "Mr. Needlemouse," *Sonic the Hedgehog* was born from a company-wide contest to take Mario down.

SEGA added the perfect element to race against Nintendo's mustachio'ed mascot: speed. *Sonic the Hedgehog* was fast, and the game felt it. With Sonic's fleet little feet came a sassy attitude, too, and SEGA had an instant hit. But an edgy mascot needs an excellent game, and SEGA delivered, featuring a beautifully designed world overflowing with fast loops, rings to collect, robots to destroy, and intricate levels that proved SEGA and Sonic had the potential to zoom past a gaming giant.

GOLDEN AXE

> YEAR: **DECEMBER, 1990**

> PLATFORM: **SEGA GENESIS/MEGA DRIVE**

> DEVELOPER: **SEGA**

> DESIGNER: **MAKOTO UCHIDA**

In a genre that had mostly featured side-scrolling street fights, *Golden Axe* offered a much-needed dose of fantasy barbarians hacking and slashing their way to bloody victory. In their quest to save the king, two brave players are challenged with taking down the evil Death Adder and his endless minions of wizards and beasts. Brawny warriors slice and destroy, as either the iconic barbarian, Ax Battler; the Amazonian Magician, Tyris Flare; or the fan-favorite, axe-wielding dwarf, Gilius Thunderhead.

From Makoto Uchida, the creator of the similarly walk-and-fight-focused *Altered Beast*, *Golden Axe* built on elements of the then-popular "side-scrolling beat 'em up" in small and fun ways, including a basic magic system, a variety of health and strength levels, dashing (and shoulder tackling), and the ever-popular rideable beasts. Finally, the dream of an angry dwarf on the back of an angrier cockatrice was made real.

ToeJam and Earl

> YEAR: **October, 1991**

> PLATFORM: **SEGA Genesis/Mega Drive**

> DEVELOPER: **Johnson Voorsanger Productions**

> CREATOR: **Greg Johnson**

What the video game world needed in 1991 was some funk, and *ToeJam and Earl* delivered it. Two blinged-out alien rappers crash-land on Earth and need to collect pieces from their spaceship in order to return to their home planet, Funkotron. As either of the constantly grooving and bopping title characters, you wander through randomly generated islands of surreal chaos, hopping out of elevators to find presents that will hopefully defend you against Earth's deplorable citizens and threats. Rogue ice-cream trucks, evil mailboxes, and swarms of nerds are just a few hazards you must navigate.

In spite of its weird veneer, the quest was oddly challenging, as neither funky space alien can do much but run away and throw tomatoes. But the difficulty level doesn't matter, so long as you're joined by a friend for a cooperative quest, which inevitably becomes hilarious and fun. It turns out that the real spirit of funk comes from partying together.

STREETS OF RAGE 2

> YEAR: **DECEMBER, 1992**

> PLATFORM: **SEGA GENESIS/MEGA DRIVE**

> DEVELOPER: **SEGA**

> PRODUCER: **NORIYOSHI OHBA**

From *Double Dragon* to *Final Fight*, there is a long and proud history of co-op games that involve walking up and down mean streets and doing karate. *Streets of Rage 2* is the beat 'em up, side-scroller's apex of bare-knuckle justice. While much of what's on offer in *Streets of Rage 2* looks familiar to anyone who has slashed through its predecessors, it's the details that set this brawler apart. Featuring a set of street warriors with top-notch names like Max Thunder, each character has unique special moves. Other improvements include new weapons, enemy life gauges, a thumping soundtrack, and gameplay that feels perfectly tuned.

But what truly sets this game apart is its colorfully realized dystopian setting. Whether smashing skulls in a dilapidated baseball field or cracking knuckles at a broken-down arcade, *Streets of Rage 2* stands tall and swings hard as one of the greatest side-scrolling, beat 'em ups ever made.

Mortal Kombat 2

> Year: **September, 1994**

> Platform(s): **SEGA Genesis/Mega Drive, Super Nintendo Entertainment System, plus others**

> Developer: **Midway Games**

> Designer: **Ed Boon**

"Get over here!" *Mortal Kombat 2* took every vicious kick and bone-snapping punch that its controversial predecessor executed and turned them up 11 notches. The resulting bloodbath is one of the most fun and ridiculous games ever made. In this legendary 2D fighting game, you don the role of one of 12 otherworldly ninjas and brawlers in order to do battle in the fantastical dimension of Outworld, where the likes of Raiden, Sub-Zero, and Johnny Cage vie to disembowel or behead one another for the honor of slaying Emperor Shao Kahn.

Where the original became known for being a combination of accessible gameplay and gruesome, match-ending fatalities, the sequel added endless new violent combinations and twists such as "babalities" and "friendships," as well as many tweaks for an all-round better game. Released across multiple home consoles and finding success everywhere it landed, the debate of which system had the best version was for many a deciding factor in the "Console Wars," and because SEGA's brought the blood it often won.

NBA JAM

> YEAR: **MARCH, 1994**

> PLATFORM(S): **SEGA GENESIS/MEGA DRIVE,**
> **SUPER NINTENDO ENTERTAINMENT SYSTEM,**
> **PLUS OTHERS**

> DEVELOPER: **MIDWAY GAMES**

> PRODUCER: **MARK TURMELL**

"He's on fire!" If you hung out in 1990s' arcades, then you knew these shouted words and you played *Jam*. *NBA Jam* was a phenomenon, and when it arrived on consoles, your friends came over and shouted those same words (and other less appropriate ones) by your side.

Jam prioritized fun, in the pursuit of which the laws of physics were incinerated alongside the majority of basketball's rules. The exaggerated 2-on-2 sports action that springs up features balls that catch fire and real-life players jumping to inhuman heights with no fouls to be found. Stirred up with properly licensed teams and players, what leapt onto consoles was one of the greatest basketball games of all time. "BOOM SHAKKA LAKKA!"

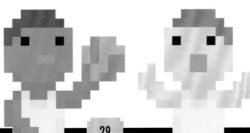

MADDEN NFL 95

> YEAR: **NOVEMBER, 1994**

> PLATFORM(S): **SEGA GENESIS/MEGA DRIVE, SUPER NINTENDO ENTERTAINMENT SYSTEM, PLUS OTHERS**

> DEVELOPER: **ELECTRONIC ARTS**

Madden has long been the reigning champion of video-game football, with a new iteration tackling the shelves nearly every year since its inception in 1989. While each sequel during the 16-bit era is layered with skull-crushing charm, it was *Madden NFL 95* that broke through the line with one simple inclusion—the names of actual NFL players and teams.

And with that, the dream of licensed football games was as real as a fumble on a Sunday. *Madden NFL 95* also established a deeper playbook than its predecessors, separating itself from the pack and establishing the series as the unstoppable blitz that it still is today.

NHL '94

> YEAR: **MARCH, 1993**

> PLATFORM(S): **SEGA GENESIS/MEGA DRIVE, SUPER NINTENDO ENTERTAINMENT SYSTEM, PLUS OTHERS**

> DEVELOPER: **ELECTRONIC ARTS**

> CREATORS: **MICHAEL BROOK, MARK LESSER**

The debate over which is the finest of the 16-bit era ice hockey games has inspired gloves-off fistfights for generations. The 1990s were a golden age for simulated sports, none more so than ice hockey, which transformed Electronic Arts into the monster of sports giants that it is today. With ice hockey, there was something about the three-quarter camera perspective and speeding your players up and down the simulated 16-bit ice rink that inspired the perfect simulation of a much grander thing.

And while the pure simplicity of *NHL '93* still deserves applause, and the subtraction of fighting and blood in '94 bruised the hearts of enthusiasts everywhere, it's the addition of goalie control, flip passes, and, more than anything else, real NHL teams and players that body-checks other hockey games out of the way. Just don't pick the Blackhawks; Roenick is way too good.

SUPER NINTENDO ENTERTAINMENT SYSTEM/SUPER FAMICOM

RELEASE DATES:

> JAPAN: **NOVEMBER, 1990**

> NORTH AMERICA: **AUGUST, 1991**

> UK AND OTHER COUNTRIES: **1992**

In the 1980s, the Nintendo Entertainment System (NES) brought the gaming industry back to life. However, a new decade dawned and, with it, a new age of gaming… and conflict. SEGA's more powerful alternative to the NES, the Genesis/Mega Drive had already been available for two years, and it wasn't alone—other systems such as the TurboGrafx-16 and forthcoming Neo Geo were encroaching upon Nintendo's dominance, all of them featuring higher-powered threats to Nintendo's aging 8-bit king. In 1990, Nintendo's Super Famicom took Japan by storm, and in 1991 the Super Nintendo Entertainment System (SNES) landed in the States and the "Console Wars" heated up in earnest. The SNES arrived late to the battle, but Nintendo's 16-bit warrior came out swinging. SEGA focused its tactics on highlighting the Genesis's edginess, calling Nintendo out in various ad campaigns for their out-dated, family-friendly nature. Nintendo returned fire, leaning into their already robust catalog of beloved games to capture the hearts of gamers. The Super Nintendo, like its contemporaries, featured more colors and better graphics than its 8-bit predecessor, but, rather than relying on arcade ports and licenses, Nintendo transformed their most successful franchises—Mario, Zelda, and Metroid—into even deeper experiences. Each of these games is regarded as being among some of the greatest in console history.

As a secondary wave of attack, Nintendo introduced new properties and franchises like StarFox, Mario Kart, and F-Zero, adding many new weapons to their already-powerful arsenal of games. In the end, what was dubbed a war between companies only benefited gamers, as diversity in the industry brought higher-quality games to the table from both companies. The competition also provided the space for other console-makers to join the fray, leaving both sides vulnerable to future assaults...

Super Mario World

> Year: **November, 1990**

> Platform: **Super Nintendo Entertainment System**

> Developer: **Nintendo**

> Producer: **Shigeru Miyamoto**

> Director: **Takashi Tezuka**

Two years late to the 16-bit party, Nintendo was ready to face-off SEGA and enter the "Console Wars," but they needed their all-star plumber to lead the charge. If *Super Mario Bros. 3* set the standard for platformers, then *Super Mario World* raised that lofty bar. *Super Mario World* transported gamers to a gorgeously saturated new corner of the Mushroom Kingdom that begged to be explored. From the rolling hills of Donut Plains to the spooky trees of the Forest of Illusion, *Super Mario World* reveled in the SNES's newfound processing powers. It featured bigger, more varied worlds to discover, all filled with countless secrets to reveal.

And no Mario game would be complete without a new set of power-ups—*Super Mario World* introduced players not only to the high-flying cape, but also to everyone's favorite, insatiable, egg-laying dinosaur, Yoshi. *Super Mario World* set a new standard for Nintendo's tremendous franchises during the 16-bit era, and Mario's (and Nintendo's) adventures would never be the same again.

EARTHBOUND

(JAPANESE RELEASE: MOTHER 2)

> YEAR: **JUNE, 1995**

> PLATFORM: **SUPER NINTENDO ENTERTAINMENT SYSTEM**

> DEVELOPER: **Ape/HAL LABORATORIES**

> PRODUCERS: **SHIGESATA ITOI, SATORU IWATA**

EarthBound defies description. Unique in many ways, this RPG (role-playing game) was a bit of an ambitious flop when it was released, crumbling under a market that wasn't ready for the genre or the game's ambition. But time has treated this strange gem well—a dedicated fan base saw past an unfavorable marketplace, and over the years its cult following blossomed into a well-deserved place alongside Nintendo's many classics.

Aside from its unlikely suburban setting, on the surface *EarthBound* resembles countless other RPGs, featuring a party of characters, hit points, stores, enemies, and dungeons to explore. But as Ness's adventure unfurls, the game reveals itself to be unlike anything else—a surreal funhouse mirror of both RPG tropes and Western culture that surprises and confounds at every turn. From Ness's weapon-of-choice, the yo yo, to his short-lived, talking bumblebee guide, from its peppy soundtrack to profound sense of loneliness, *EarthBound* is its own beast, a game, story, and experience that could only exist as a video game, and one of the most memorable RPGs in history.

F-Zero

> YEAR: **NOVEMBER, 1990**

> PLATFORM: **SUPER NINTENDO ENTERTAINMENT SYSTEM**

> DEVELOPER: **NINTENDO**

> PRODUCER: **SHIGERU MIYAMOTO**

Racing games were a mainstay of both arcades and consoles in the late 1980s and early 1990s, but nearly all of them stalled out in the face of unrelenting realism. In stark contrast, *F-Zero* zoomed onto the launch of the Super Nintendo, steering the futuristic, fast-paced hover cars of our dreams right onto Nintendo's newest console. *F-Zero's* fantastical, science-fiction world was the perfect setting to showcase Nintendo's new tech, with the SNES's much-lauded scaling and rotating "Mode-7" graphics on full display amid its inventive designs.

But *F-Zero* was more than a mere tech demo, featuring iconic characters like Captain Falcon and smartly designed tracks such as Mute City and Port Town, each with an endless array of exceedingly sharp, reflex-testing turns. All of this was wrapped up in a lightning-fast game unlike anything that had gone before and which was as challenging as it was well-designed.

THE LEGEND OF ZELDA: A LINK TO THE PAST

> YEAR: **NOVEMBER, 1991**

> PLATFORM: **SUPER NINTENDO ENTERTAINMENT SYSTEM**

> DEVELOPER: **NINTENDO**

> PRODUCER: **SHIGERU MIYAMOTO**

> DIRECTOR: **TAKASHI TEZUKA**

Lightning crashes and the disembodied voice of Princess Zelda summon Link from his slumber, and a new adventure begins. *A Link to the Past* refined the formula established in the original *Zelda* to create an enduring template for fantasy adventure games that still exists and, in doing so, became one of the greatest games of them all.

While exploring a colorful overworld and dungeons is still the foundation of the game, *A Link to the Past* added a deeper story and background, as well as countless power-ups and weapons tied to progression. Our hero can now lift boulders, swim with the Zora, race through grass, spin attack, and collect fairies in jars. Series mainstays like the hook shot, Pegasus Boots, and Master Sword appeared for the first time, all in readiness for Link to enter the Dark World—a brilliant and harrowing flip-side to the map and world that opened up countless possibilities for puzzles and exploration. *A Link to the Past* is an adventure worth taking again and again.

Street Fighter 2

> YEAR: **July, 1992**

> PLATFORM: **Super Nintendo Entertainment System**

> DEVELOPER: **Capcom**

> PRODUCER: **Yoshiko Okamoto**

> DESIGNERS: **Akira Yasuda, Akira Nishitani**

It all began with the Dragon Punch. The mastery of this precise maneuver separated the kids from the adults—if you could send Ryu's fist soaring, then getting into college really didn't matter. *Street Fighter 2* established every aspect of what it is to be a 2D fighting game, and the day that it transitioned from the arcade to a home console is the day that, for many, much of their childhood in arcades slipped away.

When *Street Fighter 2* arrived, there was nothing like it. There were complex button patterns, timings, and distinct move-sets that were unheard of, and begged to be mastered. From the electric bites of Blanka to the stretched limbs of Dhalsim, each character had its own feel and style, and the one you chose was half of your identity. By the time the game arrived on the SNES, the fervor was high and, while it came to home consoles slightly watered down, its arrival was unforgettable. "Shoryuken!" would never be the same.

Super Mario Kart

> YEAR: **September, 1992**

> PLATFORM: **Super Nintendo Entertainment System**

> DEVELOPER: **Nintendo**

> PRODUCER: **Shigeru Miyamoto**

> DIRECTORS: **Tadashi Sugiyama, Hideki Konan**

Few games have inspired players to sit on a couch and play together like the enduring *Mario Kart* series. Before the release of *Super Mario Kart*, racing games were relatively common, but it was Mario's foray onto the racetrack that introduced the new subgenre of "kart racing"—an intuitive and welcome take on driving games.

In the game, players are immersed in a colorful and whimsical scenario in which items, cartoonish physics, and recognizable characters combine to create a game that is fun for all kinds of gamers. *Super Mario Kart* is also notable for being the first game to take the Mario brand and extend it beyond the confines of a running and jumping platformer, setting the stage for countless Mario-related spinoffs to come. But few have reached the feverish heights and glories of *Super Mario Kart*, whose fusion of welcoming multiplayer gameplay and recognizable characters has become an unstoppable franchise of its own. *Super Mario Kart* set the standard for what it means to sit on your couch and shake your fist at a blue shell.

StarFox

(European release: Starwing)

> Year: **March, 1993**

> Platform: **Super Nintendo Entertainment System**

> Developer: **Nintendo/Argonaut Software**

> Producer: **Shigeru Miyamoto**

> Director: **Katsuya Eguchi**

With the war for the most powerful console in full throttle, Nintendo was anxious to prove that they still had technical prowess with their SNES—so they took the battle to outer space. Deploying a mixture of 3D polygonal graphics and a packed-in "Super-fx" chip to bolster the SNES's power, with *StarFox* Nintendo crafted an unforgettable space adventure starring an endearing cast of animal characters.

Essentially an "on-rails" space-shooter, it's the details that set *StarFox* apart, featuring small tweaks like branching difficulties, a dynamic shield, quirky co-pilots, and the ability to control the speed of your ship, the unforgettable *Arwing*. Much of what works well with *StarFox* springs from its mixture of technical wizardry abutting its memorable menagerie of animal space heroes. You are the pilot, a fox called Fox McCloud, but you'll never make it through your journey without the help and/or pestering of Peppy the Hare, Slippy the Frog, and Falco the Falcon. Top it all off with a flair barrel roll and you've got the stuff of outer-space legend.

DONKEY KONG COUNTRY

> YEAR: **NOVEMBER, 1994**

> PLATFORM: **SUPER NINTENDO ENTERTAINMENT SYSTEM**

> DEVELOPER: **RARE**

> DIRECTORS: **TIM STAMPER, CHRIS STAMPER**

> DESIGNER: **GREGG MAYLES**

The great big ape called Donkey Kong was Nintendo's first claim to video-game fame, but it took the trusted developer, Rare, to bring DK from the confines of barrel-throwing villainy into legendary 3D heroics of his own. Somebody stole Donkey Kong's pile of bananas, and it's up to Donkey and Diddy Kong to travel through the jungle and reclaim their hoard. Collecting rogue bananas while riding in mine carts and shooting from barrels, *Donkey Kong Country's* ambitious look and gameplay were an instant hit.

The game arrived in the thick of the "Console Wars" and on the eve of the next generation of gaming, and it did so as an enormous critical and commercial success, bolstering the lifecycle of the SNES in its wake. Rare had succeeded in crafting a vibrant new world for one of Nintendo's treasured properties to thrive in, and so secured their legacy as one of Nintendo's greatest partners of the era, while forever leaving their mark on the Donkey Kong Series.

SUPER METROID

> YEAR: **MARCH, 1994**

> PLATFORM: **SUPER NINTENDO ENTERTAINMENT SYSTEM**

> DEVELOPER: **NINTENDO RESEARCH AND DEVELOPMENT I/INTELLIGENT SYSTEMS**

> PRODUCER: **MAKOTO KANO**

> DIRECTOR: **YOSHIO SAKAMOTO**

Super Metroid is a video game masterpiece. Refining everything that made the original *Metroid* great, *Super Metroid* transports the adventures of interstellar bounty hunter Samus Aran into a showpiece of video-game design at its finest. A balance of inspiring exploration, haunting atmosphere, finely tuned weapons, and perfectly crafted levels weave together to create a pinnacle of adventure gaming whose influence on game design is immeasurable.

Just the right amount of minimal storytelling harmonizes with the unveiling of power-ups, and players are left feeling as if they are in control of an open-ended adventure, while subtly being nudged in the right direction with every inspiring step. From Morph Ball to Mother Brain, the result is full immersion in a video game that is a true work of art.

CHRONO TRIGGER

> YEAR: **MARCH, 1995**

> PLATFORM: **SUPER NINTENDO ENTERTAINMENT SYSTEM**

> DEVELOPER: **NINTENDO RESEARCH AND DEVELOPMENT I/INTELLIGENT SYSTEMS**

> DIRECTORS: **TAKASHI TOKIGA, YOSHINORI KITASE, AKIHIKO MATSUI**

Retro or not, no list of great games is complete without the inclusion of the legendary RPG (role-playing game) *Chrono Trigger*. Created by a trio of designers dubbed "The Dream Team," *Chrono Trigger* lived up to that hype. *Chrono Trigger* separated itself by presenting a perfectly tuned fusion of RPG elements.

An ambitious time-traveling adventure that spanned from 65 million BC to 2300 AD, the monumental journey of Crono, Lucca, Robo, and friends features an evolving world, an intricate magic system, and compelling random battles. Fused with complex characters, a beautiful setting, and an unforgettable musical score by Yasunori Mitsuda, *Chrono Trigger* emerges as one of the finest role-playing games—not only a bestseller and critical smash, but also always a regular contender for one of the greatest games of all time.

PLAYSTATION

RELEASE DATES:

> Japan: **December, 1994**

> North America: **September, 1995**

> Europe: **September, 1995**

"Live in your world. Play in ours." So read the iconic advertising for the first SONY PlayStation (PS1), and eventually nearly everyone obeyed. By the late 1980s, SONY was a leader in the world of technology and hungry to get into the lucrative video-game market. They went through several half-measures and false starts, many of which placed them in tenuous partnerships with Nintendo. Unfortunately, these partnerships soured, and by the early 1990s had transformed into a bitter rivalry between the two companies that created the context for an evolution in the video-game marketplace.

SONY knew that CD-based technology could change what video games were capable of, and stood poised to take advantage of this. But they also knew that games sold systems, and with little experience in developing on their own, they reached out to many game studios who had previously lived in the shadow of SEGA and Nintendo. They granted these developers easy access to their new technology, and a wave of new games began to take shape that crashed over the gaming public.

Nintendo were late to the party with their Nintendo 64 and never caught up in terms of third-party support. Indeed, in spite of Nintendo's impressive technology and games, they could no longer keep pace with SONY's dominance, which washed the SEGA Saturn away in its wake. Eventually expanding upon Nintendo's innovative single analog stick by adding "dual stick" technology, SONY's system became the next-generation platform to beat and the standard for 3D gaming, selling more than 100 million units (an unprecedented number) and leaving most of the world playing on these for generations of consoles to come.

RESIDENT EVIL 2

> YEAR: **JANUARY, 1998**

> PLATFORM: **SONY PLAYSTATION**

> DEVELOPER: **CAPCOM**

> PRODUCER: **SHINJI MAKAMI**

Resident Evil invented survival-horror, but its sequel perfected it. In *Resident Evil 2*, you are once again a secret agent trying to take down the evil Umbrella Corp. Unfortunately for Leon Kennedy and Claire Redfield, there are hordes of shambling zombies in the way. Emerging from the confines of the terrifying mansion of *RE1* onto the eerie streets of infested Raccoon City, *RE2* expands on the formula of tasking players with limited supplies to out-maneuver the unrelenting undead. *RE2* has a smart mix of claustrophobic terror and explosive set pieces that became the standard for survival-horror for years to come.

CRASH BANDICOOT

> YEAR: **SEPTEMBER, 1996**

> PLATFORM: **SONY PLAYSTATION**

> DEVELOPER: **NAUGHTY DOG**

> DIRECTOR: **JASON RUBIN**

Nintendo had Mario and SEGA had Sonic; SONY felt that they needed a quirky character to call their own. *Crash*

Bandicoot pioneered 3D platforming alongside its rivals, leaving its titular neckless, orange hero cemented in video-game history. In his first game, Crash ambles through a series of tropical levels to jump, spin, break crates, collect gems, and chug Wumpa Fruit on his harrowing jungle road to take down Doctor Neo Cortex. *Crash Bandicoot* is remembered fondly for its colorful visuals and precise gameplay, but it also succeeded in creating a mascot for the PS1, at least for the time being.

TWISTED METAL 2

> YEAR: **OCTOBER, 1996**

> PLATFORM: **SONY PLAYSTATION**

> DEVELOPER: **SONY/SINGLETRAC**

> DESIGNER: **DAVID JAFFE**

Twisted Metal 2 (known as *Twisted Metal: World Tour* in Europe) expanded on the chaotic demolition derby greatness of its predecessor, proving that what most cars need in order to have fun are machine guns and a missile launcher. *TM2* features an array of over-the-top characters and cars driving around and blowing one another up. The sequel was an improvement, including special moves, more characters, and exceptionally well-designed maps from cities around the world. This OTT, post-apocalyptic joyride is best enjoyed with a friend as you work together to crash an evil ice-cream truck or a man strapped to two over-sized tires into the Eiffel Tower. Teamwork at its finest.

Castlevania: Symphony of the Night

> Year: **March, 1997**

> Platform: **Sony PlayStation**

> Developer: **Konami**

> Directors: **Toru Hagihara, Koji Igarashi**

At a time when 3D gaming was all anyone could think about, *Castlevania: Symphony of the Night* ably showed that 2D platforming was still able to create some of the finest games of its time. *Symphony of the Night* departed from previous games in the series, while still borrowing many of their better elements. Gone was the series-regular whip, which was replaced by swords, nun-chucks, and javelins wielded by the shape-shifting Alucard, son of Dracula. Drawing inspiration from *Zelda* and *Metroid*, Alucard must explore the huge castle, often backtracking to revisit previously inaccessible areas using new abilities.

The resulting gameplay is the root of the modern term "Metroidvania," a subgenre of exploration-based adventure games that borrows liberally from this Castlevania edition and the Metroid series. While not a commercial success initially, *Symphony of the Night* has gone on to receive well-deserved accolades and inspire many remasters and reissues. It is now considered one of the greatest and most influential of 2D exploration platformers ever created.

TEKKEN 3

> YEAR: **APRIL, 1998**

> PLATFORM: **SONY PLAYSTATION**

> DEVELOPER: **NAMCO**

> DIRECTORS: **KATSUHIRO HARADA, MASAMICHI ABE**

By 1998, the PlayStation was a force to be reckoned with, and the 3D fighting of *Tekken* had helped take it to the virtual top. From *Tekken*'s birth in arcades to its arrival on home consoles, the previous two *Tekken* games were an enormous success. *Tekken 3* arrived to become the new benchmark for 3D fighting.

Tekken's original appeal was in balancing depth along with an easy-to-pick-up-and-play fighting mechanic, but in *Tekken 3*, Namco took many risks, adding new move-sets and, most strikingly, the revolutionary ability to side-step along another axis. Despite the increased difficulty and precision, fans embraced the new experience. The brutal Heihachi, the body-slamming King, and the sword-spinning Yoshimitsu were joined by a giant bear, a tiny dinosaur, and over a dozen new challengers for one of the greatest 3D fighting games of all time.

PaRappa The Rapper

> YEAR: **November, 1997**

> PLATFORM: **SONY PlayStation**

> DEVELOPER: **SONY/NanaOn-Sha**

> PRODUCER: **Masaya Matsuura**

> ARTIST: **Rodney Greenblat**

"Kick, jump, it's all in the mind!" *PaRappa The Rapper* created a new subgenre in video games, and did so with style. Widely regarded as the first true rhythm/music game, this inventive journey fused the visions of music producer Masaya Matsuura and artist Rodney Greenblat to create an utterly unique experience.

PaRappa is a paper-cut-out dog in a beautiful and stylized paper-cut-out world. He's got to use his raps in order to traverse through challenges that keep knocking out his self-esteem in his quest to win over the flower-headed Sunny Funny. Gameplay introduced the now-common notion of following a rhythm to timed button presses. This simple but brilliant mechanic is set to raps that are at once funny, sweet, and sometimes profound. Good vibes always win out as PaRappa makes his way to the final rap battle to tell Sunny how he really feels and once again proclaim, "You gotta believe!"

Tomb Raider

> Year: **October, 1996**

> Platform: **Sony PlayStation**

> Developer: **Core Design**

> Designer: **Toby Gard**

On the edge of a 3D gaming revolution, an unlikely heroine arrived, all guns blazing—Lara Croft, *Tomb Raider*. Originally conceived as an Indiana Jones clone, Lara Croft evolved as a result of the company's need to develop a character that would stand on its own and not draw a lawsuit. They succeeded.

The original *Tomb Raider* was an enormous hit, universally praised for its combination of thrilling action, puzzle-solving, dinosaur fights, and free-roaming gameplay. But Lara Croft's celebrity soon eclipsed the game itself, as she was launched into an international stardom that would lead to countless sequels, movies, and questionable product placements. And while the franchise has had various ups and downs since its inception, there's no doubt that the daring adventure game which sparked off Lara's stardom deserved its acclaim.

METAL GEAR: SOLID

> YEAR: **SEPTEMBER, 1998**

> PLATFORM: **SONY PLAYSTATION**

> DEVELOPER: **KONAMI**

> CREATOR: **HIDEO KOJIMA**

Metal Gear: Solid was the first video-game blockbuster. While many games before it had tried to tap into a cinematic feel, none had yet cracked the code until Konami's Hideo Kojima's ambitious foray into 3D gaming splashed down. A sequel to two lesser-known (but well-regarded) 8-bit predecessors, taking *Metal Gear* into a fully immersive 3D space was just what this now legendary franchise needed to bring Kojima's ambitious and sprawling vision to fruition.

The game that emerged is widely regarded as the first true stealth adventure, but it is remembered as much for its gameplay as for its revolutionary cinematic presentation. Taking full advantage of the CD-ROM technology of the time, *Metal Gear: Solid* features multiple camera angles, a commitment to voice acting, a fully 3D environment, an orchestral score, and some inspired and varied gameplay, to create a benchmark in interactive gaming. Of course, it also features a storyline that is in equal turns engaging and wildly confusing, but which ultimately wins you over, regardless of its head-scratching moments.

Tony Hawk's Pro Skater 2

> YEAR: **SEPTEMBER, 2000**

> PLATFORM: **SONY PlayStation**

> DEVELOPER: **Neversoft**

> DESIGNERS: **Aaron Cammarata, Chris Rausch**

The original *Tony Hawk's Pro Skater* was a smash hit, and *Tony Hawk's Pro Skater 2* improved everything about the first version, crafting not only one of the greatest skateboard simulations ever, but one of the era's most beloved games. As in the original *Pro Skater*, the sequel has you string together elaborate button combos to ollie, grind, flip, and grab your way into the the role of a pro who has to move up the career ranks. As you progress, you gain cash, learn moves and combos, and unlock new decks.

Tony Hawk's Pro Skater 2 took that winning formula and added improvements such as create-a-skater and park creation, but its biggest achievement was adding the two-wheeled manual. With the manual as a part of each shredder's skating arsenal, linking bigger and crazier combos was now possible without finding endlessly long rails to grind. Combine those epic trick-links with some of the series' best stages and music, and you were in for an unforgettable ride. "Bring the noise!"

NINTENDO 64

RELEASE DATES:

> JAPAN: **JUNE, 1996**

> NORTH AMERICA: **SEPTEMBER, 1996**

> EUROPE: **MARCH, 1997**

Those who had the Nintendo 64 loved it, but it did not win the age of the "Console Wars." Nintendo's dominance in home gaming had slipped since the 8-bit days, but it was still at the top of the growing heap when the age of 3D gaming dawned. The N64 was a leap forward for Nintendo, but it was released a year behind SONY's PlayStation, and struggled to play catch-up for its lifetime.

The N64 was an enormous transformation into three-dimensional spaces for Nintendo, presenting revolutionary games like *Super Mario 64*, which offered an unprecedented sense of free movement, while managing to keep a camera and control system that gamers could still wrap their minds and hands around. And, despite how impressive Nintendo's new games looked and felt, its greatest innovation lay in its revolutionary interface. The N64's controller was a risk—bigger than anything anyone had ever seen and with more buttons than anything before it, its greatest gamble was the analog control stick plonked right in the center.

Thankfully, it worked, and the inclusion of analog sticks quickly became the standard for 3D gaming consoles. Unfortunately, its late launch, high price-point, and the shrinking commitment of outside developers began to take their toll on the house that Mario built. The N64 was the first time Nintendo had fallen from first-place position in terms of commercial success, but it was by no means a disaster. It still sold respectably well and became the home for a wide array of excellent and successful (if primarily Nintendo-made) games.

Featuring several of the era's greatest titles, the N64's legacy is one that is held in high regard, but there is no doubt that it also marked a major shift for home gaming that stole Nintendo's spotlight for many years to come.

Super Mario 64

> Year: **September, 1996**

> Platform: **Nintendo 64**

> Developer: **Nintendo Entertainment Analysis and Development**

> Producer/Director: **Shigeru Miyamoto**

> Developers: **Takashi Tezuka, Yoshiaki Koizumi**

Super Mario 64 defined 3D gaming. The release of any Mario game is and always has been cause for excitement, but *Super Mario 64* transformed everything about the series and the very concept of platform gaming. From the opening screen in which you pluck and pull at Mario's 3D face, it was clear that Mario was no longer constrained by the horizontal plane and that this journey into Princess Peach's castle would be something new.

While not the first 3D platformer, the key to the success of *Super Mario 64's* controls and design—the subtle feeling of mass and inertia and logical movement—simply hadn't been achieved before, yet somehow Nintendo had done it. Exploration in three dimensions was real, and Nintendo made the most of it, creating yet another standard for the rest of the industry to follow. Guided by a revolutionary free-moving camera, Mario could now jump, climb trees, collect stars, swim, and explore in any direction—an idea that seems commonplace now, but at the time was a gaming revolution.

GOLDENEYE 007

> YEAR: **AUGUST, 1997**

> PLATFORM: **NINTENDO 64**

> DEVELOPER: **RARE**

> DESIGNER: **MARTIN HOLLIS**

Video games based on movies have a notoriously spotty
history. *GoldenEye 007* earned the unusual distinction
of being widely regarded as far superior to its source
material. At a time when first-person shooters were almost
exclusively played on PCs, *GoldenEye* demonstrated that
the genre had legs on home consoles. In doing so, the
Bond adventure also presented a more realistic backdrop
to the first-person shooting experience, packing in new
stealth elements like strafing and crouching that would
change the genre forever.

The game that emerged is often cited as one of the
most influential of its time, setting the stage for countless
blockbuster franchises to come, though it was never
surpassed in the glory of its addictive multiplayer Death
Matches. Something about *GoldenEye* captured the
hearts and minds of a generation of couch co-op gamers,
all of whom still love sniper rifles as a result and all of
whom know that picking Odd Job is cheating.

BANJO KAZOOIE

> YEAR: **JUNE, 1998**

> PLATFORM: **NINTENDO 64**

> DEVELOPER: **RARE**

> DESIGNER: **GREGG MAYLES**

Banjo Kazooie (and its excellent follow-up, *Banjo Tooie*) represented a true refinement in 3D platforming from Rare, a developer at the top of their game. In this game, you are an anthropomorphic bear called Banjo, aided in your quest by a companion, Kazooie, a red bird who lives inside your backpack. Banjo and Kazooie must jump, roll, and soar in order to bring down the jealous witch Gruntilda and her minions. Along the way, you solve puzzles and make friends in your quest to collect as many musical notes and puzzle pieces as a bear and a bird can.

This colorful and tightly designed open- world adventure holds up as a worthy successor and advancement to what *Mario 64* brought to the table a few years before it, and *Banjo Kazooie* is still regarded as one of the finest and most influential early platform games from one of the greatest developers of the time.

WAVE RACE 64

> YEAR: **NOVEMBER, 1996**

> PLATFORM: **NINTENDO 64**

> DEVELOPER: **NINTENDO**

> PRODUCER: **SHIGERU MIYAMOTO**

> DIRECTOR: **KATSUYA EGUCHI, SHINYA TAKAHASHI**

Jet skis are fun and cool, but no one had yet made a fun and cool jet-ski video game. Leave it to Nintendo. *Wave Race 64* took the racing genre to open waters, while representing an innovative new direction for Nintendo and the N64. Featuring a fluid mixture of accurate physics, the game functioned as much as a fun racer as proof that Nintendo was ready for the next generation of consoles outside the confines of the Mushroom Kingdom. Realistic choppy waters churn as jet skis battle and race through buoys and time trials, and the result was a resounding success.

Often forgotten amid Nintendo's voluminous number of other successful properties, *Wave Race 64* stood out, showcasing the Nintendo 64 and Nintendo's ability to stretch beyond its cartoon-ish reputation and into an ocean of fun possibilities.

SUPER SMASH BROS.

> YEAR: **JANUARY, 1999**

> PLATFORM: **NINTENDO 64**

> DEVELOPER: **HAL LABORATORIES**

> CREATOR: **MASAHIRO SAKURAI**

Like a fanboy fever dream, *Super Smash Bros.* arrived to unite all of Nintendo's varied characters onto one playing field to do battle, and yet another enduring Nintendo franchise was born. Where else can Pikachu punch Mario right in the moustache? Directed by the legendary Masahiro Sakurai, *Smash* implemented many new ideas in fighting games in order to create a game that was more accessible for casual fans to pick up and play, but still offered depth to more determined players.

Instead of a standard energy bar, players are tasked with knocking one another off the iconic themed stages—most of which feature dynamic platforms and challenges of their own. Move-sets are more basic and universal than those of contemporary fighting games; instead, emphasis is placed on aerial combat and movement, as well as on an array of randomly generated weapons and power-ups. Top that off with the ability to have four players fighting at once, and a chaotic video-game classic was hatched.

THE LEGEND OF ZELDA: OCARINA OF TIME

> YEAR: **NOVEMBER, 1998**

> PLATFORM: **NINTENDO 64**

> DEVELOPER: **NINTENDO**

> PRODUCER: **SHIGERU MIYAMOTO**

> DIRECTORS: **EIJI AONUMA, YOSHIAKI KOIZUMI, TORU OSAWA, YOICHI YAMADA**

Ocarina of Time once again transformed one of Nintendo's beloved characters and franchises, and in doing so changed the landscape of adventure games. All the trappings of the original 2D *Zelda* were on full display—collection, special weapons, irritated chickens, intricate dungeons, quirky villagers—but *Ocarina* also reset the standard for what it meant to be a *Zelda* game.

One of Ocarina's many talented directors and the man considered to be the father of modern Zelda, Eiji Aonuma, said of *Ocarina*, "Every single aspect of the game was an experiment to us." A bounty of new ideas emerged, from a revolutionary targeting system and a time-bending quest to a vision of Hyrule that lived and breathed in unprecedented ways. Countless players still cite the moment they stepped onto Hyrule Fields as being one of the greatest in their gaming lives, and understandably so—*Ocarina of Time* remains an icon of adventure.

TECHNICAL SPEC

This list kept me up at night. Despite our fondest recollections, nostalgia does not always align with quality. It is my hope I've chosen games that speak both to warm fuzzy feelings and to enduring excellence. I hope this book is a good read, but also provides some fun cultural context. There are many games that deserve to be here but aren't, and there are wonderful consoles that are also nowhere to be found. In the interests of space, clarity, and effectively weaponized nostalgia, we focused on systems and games that were particularly popular and influential.

Where appropriate, I've limited the number of games from a single franchise. It's my hope that cultural impact and influence were prioritized (I just wish I could have written about *Night Trap*). Notable exceptions are industry mainstays such as *Mario* and *Zelda*, whose incremental changes made big differences to game design and gamers, and had an immeasurable impact, so they've gotten extra slots (though many important iterations are missing—sorry, lovers of *Majora's Mask*).

Another notable exception is the Game Boy and its many sequels. As one of the bestselling and longest-living gaming platforms of all time, the Game Boy's success cannot be overstated, but its list was kept deliberately short. The two games chosen were highlighted because of their enormous influence, which stemmed from their handheld birth. With all due respect to *Kirby* and the rest, while the Game Boy housed many fine games, they were very often diminutive versions of their console siblings.

In finalizing this list, I looked not only to my extensive experience as a gamer, but also to the Internet's general consensus. Inevitably, people will disagree with me. Hopefully, the games included have all stood the test of either memory or influence, maybe even both. This list comes down to my informed opinion, which has probably already changed. It hurt to choose *Chrono Trigger* over *Final Fantasy 6*, but I did. Tell me where you think I've steered the ship poorly; I'd love to hear from you.

To conclude: We salute you, SEGA Master System, SEGA Game Gear, Atari Lynx, TurboGrafx-16 (BONK!), Neo Geo, Atari Jaguar, blessed SEGA Saturn and SEGA Dreamcast, and all the rest... You gave us many great games, and we haven't forgotten you.

INDEX

ACKNOWLEDGMENTS

Thanks to my family and friends who have supported, tolerated, and indulged in my love of video games. My Dad, in particular, who even got me a SEGA-CD, an indulgence I'd possibly have been better off missing out on (but Sonic CD was REALLY good), and my older brothers and sister, who occasionally let me play Track 'n' Field.

Thanks to my first and best co-gamer for life, Jeremy Murphy, whose Street Fighter 2 prowess is matched only by his rage at only very occasionally losing a fight. And to Meclina, for having better taste in games than any of us. And the entire glorious Murphy family for feeding rampant teenagers while letting them play endlessly in their home.

And thanks to my many grown-up gamer friends: Dan Brennan, James Bernardinelli, Roarlivia, Andy Wade, Peter Maguire, Lip, 210, Thomas Stephanos, Jason Vandewalle, and anyone and everyone who has ever sat on my couch and listened to me scream about the injustice of blue shells.

Thanks to my games-writing family at Goomba Stomp—there are too many passionate writers to name, but particular appreciation goes to Ricky Da Conceicao, who keeps the lights on and steers the ship.

Thanks to my stalwart and true editor, Pete Jorgensen, who read what I wrote about Zelda and wondered if I might like to write another book. He's still the bee's knees. And many thanks to all of his fine associates at Dog 'n' Bone Books—they keep letting me write books, and I love it every time.

And thanks most of all to my wonderful little family. Our beloved pup, Whiskey, and my beautiful, talented, and endlessly supportive partner, Jocelyn Sage Mackenzie. Thanks for your songs and mind and art and tremendous and inspiring heart (and for making sure I remember to eat).

But most of all, thanks to you for playing games AND reading words about them. Get back in there, the princess is in another castle.